Heart, Breath, and Graceful Movement

Ecstatic Love Poems

by
Pamela Eakins

Wild Girl Publishing
Santa Cruz, CA 95061

Heart, Breath, and Graceful Movement

Copyright ©2006 by Pamela Eakins

Heart paintings and calligraphy by Joyce Eakins

Book and cover design by Jane Nyberg

ISBN-10: 0-9728146-1-2
ISBN-13: 978-0-972814-61-4

Library of Congress Control Number: 2006925785

This book is printed on paper that is fifty percent recycled, is acid free, and elemental chlorine free. Proceeds from sales support sustainable and joyous forests.

Published by

Wild Girl Publishing
PO Box 1301
Santa Cruz, CA 95061

For Mirabai,
I am breathed in the effulgence of your being
breathed full with the fiery presence
that brings all that is into being
and takes my breath away.

Contents

Graceful Movement

Introduction

Lover, welcome!

Lover, enter!

Enter these pages, Beloved, for who loves Love more fiercely than you? And if these poems of love were not made for you, then I know not for whom the author penned them.

Enter now the story of love divine, a sweet, erotic love story emblazoned with all the succulent, dripping nectar of religious revelation.

This is the story of Mira and Chinay – of Mira's deep desire, of Chinay's heartfelt longing.

Behold, Beloved, the deep struggle of these lovers. Behold their torment, behold their pain. Behold, likewise, the apex of their ecstasy. Attend well. Read aloud and slowly – even as if you are waking to love yourself. For who are these two lovers if not our own selves waking; who are they if not our own selves being born?

Beloved, this is who we are: We are Love seeking Love, Love with wonder gazing into Love's own love-struck eyes.

Here we are Beloved, entwined in the heart of Love – you and me – together now, risen in ecstasy, forever born again in the fire of creativity.

The Players

Two Lovers:

Mira: She who looks, reflects, seeks a miracle. Sometimes she grasps that the miracle has occurred. Sometimes she is blind to magnificence, though the whole of the cosmos glistens in blinding illumination.

Chinay: Creator, maintainer, and destroyer of worlds. He who is awakened by Love, is captivated. He who – burgeoning with love, and feeling incomplete as never before – seeks a way into wholeness. Sometimes he is a man to Mira. Sometimes He is a god. Always, he/He is Love, all that is Holy.

Heart

Mira stands on the edge

Mira stands on the edge of the abyss
She is praying with a milagro
for the assistance of gods

Holding the metal heart in her hand
she raises it like a lightning rod

See this heart? she cries
It is already stricken!

Chinay says she struck him
like a thunderbolt

Who electrified whom?
They are both electrified

Mira prays
to be
shattered.

milagro: a metal charm placed on an altar to help create a miracle

Her sister says Chinay is her heartbeat

Her sister says
Chinay is her heartbeat
the pulse of the world
the rhythm of wind blowing
water falling mountain rising
bright comet sailing back
through black skies of summer

He is her dark obsession –
Lord of hot desire
her breath her blood her blessing

Chinay is the blood
pressing through her veins
blessing that girl
inside her arteries
rivers of birds surge flying
with red-winged passion
swooping up from ashes
into cosmic fire.

Mira says Chinay is the Holy One

Mira says
Chinay is the Holy One
He is the unmanifest god
made manifest
then disappearing again

She says
He comes to the door
and I am at the threshold
falling

She says
Do you hear?
When he comes in
My heart stops
When he goes out
My heart stops

Mira cries out over rooftops in the village
Am I living
Or dying
to love?

Mira says When I am with him

Mira says
When I am with him
hours pass
like the ancient river
without beginning
or end
flowing into the sea

When I am without him
I hear the old clock ticking
time passing waiting
seconds moving like geologic time
my beating heart
waiting longing waiting
to become one again in the timeless river

Mira moves without past or future
in the parallel universe of
   Chinay.

Chinay calls again

Chinay calls again says *I never
give up*
Mira races
Thank God she cries
Chinay!

Her heart is on fire for her lover
She is burning in ecstasy
tormented with longing
crazed that she will lose him
trembling with impassioned madness
at the curvature
of his honey almond eyes

She has tasted his tears
swallowed his laughter
drunk sweet nectar from
the fountain beneath his tongue
and now she sits dazed
pondering
wondering
the name of the path that leads to
      Forever.

Her heart her hearth her home

Her heart her hearth her home
her fire
Mira would tear her heart out
and place it on the pyre for
Chinay

Supplicant nun
Mira yearns to enfold to embrace
enrapt to hold
to be entered by Chinay
as the heart of the bodhisattva
enters bodhicitta

Serving chela
she wants to feed him grapes
like the mother bird feeds the baby
craves the feel of his fluttering heartbeat
soft fledgling wings brushing downy twigs
on the inside
of her nest.

chela: a disciple, a student, a devotee

Mira said she imagined Chinay drinking

Mira said
she imagined Chinay drinking
from her neck

Drinking from her neck?

What can that mean?

It means she imagined
that he had won her
taken her

He had taken her heart
held it in his trembling hand
and he was now planting sharp kisses
on her jugular vein.

Mira rushes into Chinay

Mira rushes into Chinay
like a child pushes wildly
into the sea
not knowing the power
the tumult, the churning
naïve to the current
the riptide the gathering
the dispersal

Mira rushes into sea
drowns tumbled under succumbing to
the vastness of his being
her heart, pounding madly
like crashing waves against the jetty
rolls like thunder rippling on the shore

Wavelike, she swells to rise
rolls and curls
and dies once more.

Chinay says the image

Chinay says the image
of Mira flows through him ceaselessly
her eyes – the color – her eyes
her ocean eyes exploding into
kaleidoscopic infinity

Mira's heart shatters in
a hundred thousand places
She breaks like the sea
collapses in ecstasy
spirals over breathlessly
into her own yearning embrace

She reaches out to grasp the air and water
of sacred desire
and all of it –
rushing sea and spray, froth and foam –
rages flimsily passing
through her grasping hands
as she struggles to hold that
which refuses to be
contained.

Chinay's presence is always

Chinay's presence is always with her
He says he is rushing headlong
toward her
leaping like the waterfall leaps
plunging over the cliff-edge

Mira is awash in ecstasy
pooling in the place at the base
where torrent meets ground
dissolving in the alchemical transformation
of Chinay

When she thinks of him – she swoons
It is ecstasy, despair, unbearable
beauty, sorrow insufferable, radiant
innocence and innocence lost
the intense light and darkness of loving
the Holy One forever

Before she knew Him she had
no idea she was alone
Now He passes like a holy current
through her supplicated breast
in a sudden moment of remembrance
while she is washing her hair.

Chinay writes Even more complex

Chinay writes *Even more complex*
Now I not only think of you
moment by moment
but have to hold myself
back from calling you
time after time

Mira is gone
she is over the edge
she is over the edge in ecstasy
languishing
in the place where her secret god
has entered the fallow chambers
of her heart

He stands waiting
she is howling at the moon

Her wild heart once dormant
now pounds out the rhythm
of his bloodstream

Her wild heart pounds the rhythm
of the stream of being
from the end of this world
to the inception of the next.

Mira is mad with love

Mira is mad with love for Chinay
balmy in her devotions
How will this end, she wonders
and yet she deludes herself

There is no end
no beginning
no future and no past
She deludes herself madly
thinking that there is a goal

He is Who Is, Has Been, Shall Become
and Shall Be
merely holy fire in holy water
in the endless cosmic sea.

Note: Goals and gods are sometimes interchangeable.

Chinay is sailing through

Chinay is sailing through hidden chambers
between high sailing clouds
in the deep dark black of night

Mira is in her coracle flying night skies
seeking hidden realms
of desire in secret dreams
of that star-clad empire
where she believes Chinay must reside

She dreams he knows her well
but she knows him not
not where he lives
nor eats nor sleeps nor sails
not where he drops anchor in that dark estate
at the edge of some remote
paradisiacal isle

She knows him better though
than she might surmise
Guided by stars in the girl's love-struck eyes
he sails and anchors his godly arts
in the endless trembling oceanic chambers
of cosmic Mira's
dream-filled
heart.

Chinay says with each moment

Chinay says with each moment
I become more deeply you
We become in every moment
more deeply *us*

Mira is dwelling on the *we-ness, us-ness,*
the merged togetherness
of loving *Chinay*

How it feels *being* with Chinay
How it feels *becoming* with Chinay
How her life now is the life
of a devotee a supplicant

How she worships
the red road He walks on
stalks Him at temple
places garlands at His shrine

She is mad
with singing praises
raises His banner
marks His symbols on her door

She is devoted now
Chinay says *You are mine*
Now Mira rests in madness
knowing Love's the soul of time.

Chinay reaches lovingly

Chinay reaches lovingly
toward Mira's face

Mira has the impulse to
take His fingers in her mouth
and bite His hand
– a strange communion

Don't get too close to the cage
Chinay
stay back from the bars
the edges

This Mira may seem tame
but she is on fire
and every fiber of her being
wants to envelop you

She wants to eat you Chinay
stay away
from the edges
She desires you Chinay –
stand back from
the cell.

Oh my heart!

Oh my heart!
Do not rise up as a witness against me!
When I stand before the tribunal
judged at last by the Infinite Powers
Will you, Most Light, testify on my behalf?
or will you, Most Heavy, make a dark case
against me and condemn me to
eternal damnation?

Be it known that my love for him
was innocent
Be it known that my love for him
was pure
Be it known that in Him I sought eternal salvation
for He was all eternity, vivified
in the center of my soul

This, Mira called out in her dream
and when she awakened
innocence and purity, dark knowledge and prurity
washed over her like a raging waterfall
as she was baptized, flesh and blood,
in the raging flood of
Chinay.

I have so little to give you

I have so little to give you Holy One
said Mira
and I want to give you –
           all my life

I have words, just words, words of song
mantra prayer
and I have my heart
this heart this Mira's heart of love flooding
and I have this body this flesh and blood –

She could not continue, broke off
began to weep
and Chinay like a mirror wept
an endless river
could not stop weeping

The beggar girl, though, did not know
gods could cry this way
Was it just for what she was saying
or was it god-like sorrow expressed in just
the moment He was
wafting away?

Chinay spoke softly Death

Chinay spoke softly *Death*
comes if you leave me death
comes if you stay

Gods are transformed by worship
as penitents are changed by gods

Mira's heart is volcanic
raising new chains of islands
in the netherworld of oceans
each vestige a prayer

My heart my heart she cries
breaking and aching
I have witnessed love in the Lord's eyes
burst through obstacles in
my own illusive devotions
encountered the wrenching suffering of gods
and now I am dying living
in Love's domain
this Mira's heart enfolded
in a cup of quantum pain.

Chinay says he cannot sleep

Chinay says
he cannot sleep

He sleeps like a village
besieged by enemies
watching waiting one eye open
waiting for his Lover
though he knows she will not come

His Mira is far away
across a bay and over mountains
weeping for him on a severed stump
in a place where her own mortal enemy
now resides
and a strong tide once touching edges
recedes.

Note: Mira's own worst enemy is herself.

Is it life or death

Is it life or death
to know Love?

The heart breaks open
blood flooding like sea
becomes a watery marsh
where tides fall and rise and
blue herons wade
ducking for dark creatures
everybody swallowed whole

Mira's body is an estuary
a safe stop on Chinay's migration

She keeps the sanctuary open
day by day waiting
for her blue god to arrive
to wing in and drink down
her dark offerings –
        whole, salty and
        near the surface.

Breath

When Chinay and Mira locked eyes

When Chinay and Mira locked eyes
the two halves of their broken symbolon merged

Every reigning myth was shattered
pairs of shutters to the infinite parted

Chinay whispered
I have been searching for you Mira
for ten thousand lifetimes

Mira closed her eyes and shuddered
breathing
I only now realize
that I lost you Holiness –
ten thousand lifetimes
ago.

Chinay says Look at the sky

Chinay says
Look at the sky and the ocean!

It's a Rothko painting!
Orange and blue stripes!

Mira says
The orange sky is touching
the blue sea
                Everywhere

Mira says
I am the sea
and you are the sky Chinay

I am undulating
and you are kissing me
                Everywhere.

Chinay says I have lost

Chinay says
I have lost my bearings
my bearings dissolved
my foundation is liquefied
I am the breath of sky merging with
the ocean of Mira
gold eyes seeing silver
seeing silver seeing gold
infinite reflection
my eyes in her soul

Mira is swooning
she is ocean
in the breathing infinite sky-field of Chinay
she has lost her sense of gravity
and does not know which way is which

The multiplication of him
is her North Star
and her mind has become
        convoluted.

Sister, He is the Sun

Sister,
He is the Sun

To look into his eyes too long
is to be blinded

When I am with him
there is no time
and there is no space

Everything stops

They say that is what death is
        – stopping like that

This love must be death then
breath stopping
for I am looking on the face of God

And they say no one can
look upon the face of God

       and *live.*

Chinay says You are the ocean

Chinay says *You are the ocean Mira*
undulating with intelligence
and wisdom and knowledge
writhing with the undulating
waves of the intelligence
of the sea

Mira thinks *You are a god*
the god of sea and sky sun and earth
god turning galaxies and ancient stars
blue stars flaring forth
He who is giving birth
to Mira
sevadol in the shrine of Chinay

Mira is forever transformed
since Holiness entered her temple
singing mantras of Love
beneath His breath.

sevadol: gracious server

Mira sees Chinay's face

Mira sees Chinay's face in
the thousand cranes flying by
her window

Their kinetic configuration
is the bliss of Chinay – his trepidation
his sorrow his ecstatic revelation
His holy kiss

Chinay says Mira never looks the same
that she changes with the light
like infinite expressions
of twilight folding into seamless night

What moving river
dropped these two lovers
into the flowing ocean
of one another's eyes?

What kinetic windstream
bound them in freefall
through the unbounded chasm
of one another's sighs?

Mira writes to Chinay

Mira writes to Chinay
There is that place of moving through membranes
deeper and deeper
and deeper until
you find that place
of touching luscious center
that place from which love's gushing
river spills

Chinay's breath thickens
He falls from his chair
to his knees
to his side on the ground
shakes his head
feeling shock waves rubs his forehead
Reeling, he reasons *She is just who she seems*

Mira half wakens to a jolt from Chinay
surging with heat amidst disjointed scenes
      Being in love is living
      in the center of quaking ecstasy
      Being in love is living
      in the core of
      fiery dreams.

Cormorants open their wings

Cormorants open their wings
on the shore
stand like totems
of greeting and warning
drying out the night mist
in the morning of the day

They can move in split seconds
flit dance dive
but, Mira, hapless beggarwoman
madwoman bondwoman nun
stands still like a hummingbird
hopeful heart fluttering still
waiting endless aeons
for the Holy One to come.

Ravished, craven, Mira paces

Ravished, craven, Mira paces the beach
blown back by the storm
sea and salt spray flying
mist dying into rain
wet with passion
she craves Chinay
cannot release him from her belly

Ravin she would consume him
like prey
take Him inside her
make her body from His
His life becoming her
her body becoming His
she would dissolve Him
at once disappear
all life merging as
light swallows light
and the universe folds back
into itself.

Searching for an omen

Searching for an omen
Mira watches seagulls spread their wings
flap and rise from the rocky reef
as stampeding ghost mustangs
of froth and water
careen phantomlike wash and die
over ledges

I could rise like that, she thinks,
fly with ease from this tumult

Chinay has given me wings
bound me with cosmic breath
to push against

Maybe that's why I love him
because He lifts me from darkness
Maybe that's why I want to fly away
because when He leaves I fall in darkness
stunned, stumbling, and
utterly blind.

Letters of flame burn

Letters of flame burn the ground
and reach skyward
rising like the phoenix in transmutation
Mira drops in exultation
making her self the offering whispering
  Te adoro

The Holy One is everywhere
breathing seeking reaching feeling
for shards of recognition
signs of free volition
winged offerings freely given
rising to meet His open grasp
Like a hawk he hunts
his chela

Mira lies upon the earth waiting
her life rife with scarlet passioned
ribbons of silence calling
Come Holiness, take me
Yo   Te adoro
Te necesito
Yo   Te amo
Yo Te quiero

She longs to die into the mystic stream
of wind currents howling
inside the hallowed dream.

Mira whispers Are you with me

Mira whispers *Are you with me, Holiness?*
She can feel His Sacred Presence
like heightened air all around her
and in the cool of twilight devotions
her hair stands on end
like a stand of redwoods on hallowed land
at land's end

She goes silent, prayer beads in hands trembling
heart aflame
the nape of her neck cold as black ice

She becomes the quaking surface of chaos
reflecting Heaven then exploding
heavenward
parting waters for rushing sky
She is volcanic fissure
egg smashed burst open
breaking to become fluid surrender
vanquished and blasted away
Ancient cliffs no longer holding
she is screaming out
      Chinay!

Chinay entered Mira's temple

Chinay entered Mira's temple
surprised Mira at worship
She gasped in the sudden recognition
of the sweetness of Him in the doorway
almost too much for her to bear

She offered Him water
and He tipped the glass over
spilling sweet water on earth
in a symbolic rite
that purified the wanting
satiated longing
consecrated the foundation
and laid the cornerstones
for a new way of knowing
to ascend

Water poured on
ancient scriptures
and
nothing
was lost.

When Chinay entered the shrine

When Chinay entered the shrine
Mira dissolved in ultimacy

He leaned through the doorway
she felt the rush and tumble of intimate presence
gasped in awe and sheer delight
at the surprise of Him
and disintegrated in ecstasy

Mira calls out through the aeons
          yes yes yes yes
The Holy One has arrived
and I am entreating Him

He arrives after ten thousand lifetimes
and I have opened wide the jade
gate.

The Holy One asks Where is bread

The Holy One asks *Where is bread*
for the wine?

Mira sips wine from His mouth
offers bread from her lips
bows at the altar
remembering
His holy decrees

Placing fruit and offerings
Thy Will – she whispers breathlessly
Eat and be strong, Holiness
Eat, breathe, live,
that I may love you
       – Sacred Presence –
just one more precious day.

Mira is crying for Chinay

Mira is crying for Chinay
He has loved her
made love to her
taken her in his embrace
and loved her more deeply
than she has ever
been graced by Love before

The Holy One is a lover
breath beyond breathing
effulgent beyond effulgence
this Mira
has ever known

He has enfolded her
she has enfolded him
and now she understands Destiny

Now she knows Divinity
She has entered the temple
and her passion has been
reborn.

Mira is a nun on fire

Mira is a nun on fire
She inhales ethers from the fiery cosmos
exhales prayers mantras versicles
implores the Holy One
to enter her shrine
to eat and drink her offerings
to taste the banquet she has laid before Him
to own the blood and pumping
in her own sacred heart

She is mad for the Divine
mad for the Holy One
mad for heartfire flaring heavenward
firebirds flaring from smoking ash

She is crazy and pure, brash and demure
with longing loving wanting
Holiness to claim her
as she has claimed Him
bound Him tied Him yoked Him to her altar
if only in His image, if only in her dreams

If He would enter her sanctuary
        she would fall at His feet
If He would inhabit her statuary
        her life would be complete.

Chinay says I heard you praying

Chinay says *I heard you praying Mira*
I heard your voice
whispering novenas
singing matins
before the dawn

You invoked me enticed me
drew me to you with your
supplications
and now I claim you
temple bride of the congregation
that your worship
may last forever

This is a mystery from the
dawn of Creation:
What is a god who is not invoked?
What is a mendicant without invocation?

Chinay says he is in torment

Chinay says he is in
       torment
that if she should leave him
he would be – *in misery*

That he would be drained of
       the last drop of energy
that he would be a lifeless husk
       become living dead
ask himself how long this state
       might last

Because he knows it would be
       permanent

Without his Mira
He could not bear the thought
of trying to teach
anyone about Love

       ever again.

Mira tries to sneak downstairs

Mira tries
to sneak downstairs
so her housemate will not hear her

She wants wine –
sweet Dionysian mystery

because Chinay has entranced her
and she is begging now for

      mercy.

Graceful
Movement

Sister, the Man is a river

Sister,
the Man is a river
If you look deep in his eyes
you see silver salmon running
climbing ledges
desperate to spawn

He has taken me
to the inside ledge of the outer edge
of existence
And I am awash in those waters
an iridescent fish in luminous breeding ground
the infinite round of being
where I have found
my
mission.

Chinay meets Mira by the water

Chinay meets Mira by the water
He multiplies Himself for the world
lets all the maidens love Him
but the blue god says He was
made man for Radha

He says that only Radha's stick
pounding the sanctum floor
can waken the power of fiery creation
in His smoldering white-hot core

In right times His holy script
flows outward like a river –
in wrong times even gods despair
of ever finding truth

Mira, His Radha,
bangs her muse stick on the roof
and a snaking patterned lava flow
burns Writ on Holy Ground

For this, Chinay is eternally grateful
   – he was two times lost –
      but now he's
         found.

Radha: the God of Love's most beloved lover

Chinay told Mira Sometimes

Chinay told Mira
Sometimes I idealize you

But there are other times
when I see you
just as you are

> *A woman*
> *tracing the flow of my letters*
> *with your fingernail*
> *across the page*

Just that
Nothing more

Yet such movement can fling me –
> *love is madness*
> *sweet madness –*
> > *deep erotic encounter –*
far beyond the dark side
of the
> *moon.*

Chinay says Even the mountain

Chinay says
Even the mountain ranges
can all be made
magma again

All this molten rock
is us, Mira

No bearings –

Just power
seeking
            form.

Chinay writes I would toss

Chinay writes
I would toss her pink sweater
to the side
where it would fall
inevitably
on her reams and reams of love poems

And this lover
this poet
this woman of passion
mad with longing
would not be speaking

now.

Chinay said Mira write

Chinay said *Mira write the words*
        'unbearable sweetness'
because that is what I feel
when I am in the shrine
and I see your face
looking up at me

Mira writes
        unbearable sweetness
with a stick in wet sand
where a high tide
covered the beach
only four hours earlier

Mira thinks *so sweet*
so unbearable
writing secrets between waves
She laughs like the madwoman's daughter
because Chinay has slipped
through her fingers
like water
once again.

Unbearable sweetness breathes

Unbearable sweetness breathes Chinay
That is sacred bliss at the center
of the universe

Wrapping you in primal devotion
I am the ocean of love, Mira
surging from the heart of the cosmos
imploding your chela's brow and heart
in fiery resolution
igniting sacred spark
sacred bliss and catalytic genesis
a white-hot awakening
through the unbearably tender kiss
of dissolution

You sought me, Mira
I am He who casts you asunder
your cataclysmic annihilation
the answer to your prayerful ablutions
the soul of the freedom
you are yearning to receive

I come to rend the veils
of your efforts to perceive –
and by this hot blade through your heart, Mira
you will open to conceive.

Mira says This is not

Mira says *This is not*
the generic Mira
applied to Chinay
Black-clad sister Mira
died December's third day
and went straight to caterpillar heaven

This Mira wraps Chinay
in wings of gold gossamer
feeds Him ambrosia from her ancient cup
nectar through honeyed lips parting
sings to Him ecstatic canticles
evoking the remembrance
of Love's sacred fires coursing

This Mira is your lover your mother your child
your chela your devotee your novice your nun
This Mira is your mage maga imago
dissolved in the screaming logos
having made Love's fire her home.

maga: priestess

54

In her dream Mira had a son

In her dream
Mira had a son with
Down's Syndrome

He was Love incarnate
but in the dream
the family could not comprehend –

They would not let him enter the picture
they were making for the silver frame

But then Mira's love for Chinay
does not fit known borders

Such boundless simple sweet devotion –

Only a Golden Love Child
could issue forth
from the endless flaming ocean of
their love.

Chinay says I'm way swept off

Chinay says
I'm way swept off the ledge
of my former life
already fused with her
like that hole that wraps around the pink button
how the pink button
slips inside the hole

And my fingers betray me
trembling with fierce attention
trying to be suave so cool
I cannot undo the maddening layers

Yet I am already

inside.

Time stopped when Chinay

Time stopped when Chinay
came into Mira's holy shrine

Had she adored Him so well
that He assumed human form?

Everything ended as one plus one
made one

Had she died in that
moment
– she would have been
          complete.

Chinay encountered Mira

Chinay encountered Mira
in her devotions
eyes closed tight
soft tears rolling down the side of her face

What's wrong, Mira?
he asked softly
kissing the salty rivulets
flowing into her hair

Mira began to sigh and weep
the tide no longer contained
inside her

Sometimes pain looks like ecstasy, Chinay
sometimes ecstasy is mistaken for

     pain.

Already now Mira says

Already now, Mira says,
when you leave me Chinay it takes
so long to return to equilibrium

I go through tumultuous layers
the most immense joy
          – an intensity of life
the most immense grief
          – an intensity of death
greater than I have ever known

Then, for a time, equilibrium
is only the exact balance
between laughter and tears
until I become quiet and sensible
and surrender to the knowledge
that what is, is
and to wish otherwise is
an equation for the most
immense suffering.

Chinay says Now is a time

Chinay says *Now is a time*
when I want to be with you
Every now has that quality
surging into its one moment
and all I want about now
is that you be in it
with me
At the same time I want to
reflect with you on all your
reflections
on our confluence
on rivers that join
and erode mountains

Mira is rushing toward him
white water careening through arroyos
and up the sides of painted hills

How can a river rush up hill?
Ask any question –
Love is the answer.

The lovers cleave around

The lovers cleave around
the knife edge of Zain
wanting waiting yearning
feeling the pain of separation

The Holy One needs His devotee
the chela needs her Teacher

Who gives power to whom?
Who is the center?
Is not the inside of everything One?

The lovers delude themselves
thinking they are separate
they are one being
cleaving
in the infinite name of
Love.

Zain: a letter of the Hebrew alphabet symbolizing sword,
curiously often associated with lovers.

Mira says I am who has

Mira says *I am who has sought Chinay*

He sought me, found me,
fit me, made me whole
and we are like a broken pot mended

He adhered me to Him
drew a glaze around us
and catalyzed my broken pieces into
something other
than I have previously been

Now I can contain
what poured over me wastefully
like honey tipped over
on the kitchen floor.

When Chinay touched Mira's lips

When Chinay touched Mira's lips
with His infinite kisses
Mira sailed into stars

With each kiss she could see
the edges of a galaxy being born
spirals sparkling twinkling
enfolded in black velvet
each bejeweled cluster turning majestically
and in turn becoming the very heart
of the royal universe itself

Each kiss is holy
births and bears expanding star systems
holds all the cosmos in orbit
pledges into place the heavenly plan

If lovers do not kiss, I ask you,
Who will ensure that the world whirls,
that baby stars flare forth to light Love's eyes
as the akasha of Love unfurls?

If lovers do not kiss
who will assure continuation –
if not Love loving Love's
empyrean creation?

akasha: the subtle ether that pervades the universe

Chinay is Mira's muse

Chinay is Mira's muse
If she should lose Him
through merging in oneness becoming one
or in twoness becoming too
far removed
for whom would she consecrate her altar?
To whom would she dedicate her sacred vow?

Does Mira's longing and yearning
for that which is in her
serve?

Chinay has been with her
from the beginning,
will be inside her for all time –

Ash to ash
He shifts His disguise
and she is a red bird rising from ashes,
with visions of enchantment in her eyes.

Chinay says she struck him

Chinay says
she struck him like a thunderbolt
that he was walking the world
like water
and he saw her
and she was potassium
and he touched her
and they exploded
exploded together
became suddenly everywhere
blasting through the matrix
of Indra's web

Everywhere nowhere endless infinite
the two lovers flow
dead and borne in the massive transmutation
of Love's cataclysmic conflagration.

Indra: the supreme God of Fire and Wind

Chinay said He came to peace

Chinay said He came to peace
when Mira told Him
she would never leave Him
that He would never be alone in the deepest
darkest
places
again

Even gods need to know they are not
alone

Even gods need to know that they have
a home
in the endless eternal breath
of forever.

Acknowledgements

Thank you to the following people who helped make this book possible:

Elizabeth Beauchamp, Lucia Birnbaum, Lisa DiPlacido, Melody Culver, Ratna Jennifer Sturz, Kathleen Donovan, Joyce Eakins, Carolyn Brigit Flynn, Loren Foster, Kathy Hall, Linda Hennessy, Milicent Kari, Judith Dempsey Malear, Sue Martin, Cynthia McDonald, Jane Nyberg, Louann Pironti, Fay Rohrbach, Gaël Roziére, Douglas Snow, Charlene Spretnak, Gary Swartzman, Brian Swimme, Akasa Tseng, Pamela Wylie, and Betty Zographos.

About the Author

Anciently of the Clan Eakins of the Isle of Skye, Pamela Eakins is a scribe, sculptor, minister, professor and peacemaker. She has taught at the University of Colorado, Stanford University, and the California Institute of Integral Studies. She holds a doctorate in sociology from the University of Colorado. Pamela founded Pacific Center in 1990 where she teaches courses dedicated to personal  transformation, cosmological understanding, and practices of peace. She is the author of *Tarot of the Spirit, Priestess, The American Way of Birth* and *Mothers in Transition.* Her mission is peacemaking and social change through the one true path – the quest for eternal Love. Visit her web site at www.pamelaeakins.org.

Photo by Ryan Schubert

About the Publisher

Wild Girl Publishing was born in 2000 at a writing retreat in the Santa Cruz Mountains. In that beautiful place, I reconnected to the wild girl in me – the one who ran free chasing the wind, the one who climbed into treetops and made trails through empty lots, the one who boldly spoke her mind, the one who knew she belonged on earth. This wild girl is jubilantly happy to be recognized once again.

From this joy was born the idea of publishing books to encourage each of us to find the wild one in ourselves. May we all grow to recognize our own wild souls.

Jane Nyberg
Santa Cruz, California

Wild Girl Publishing
PO Box 1301
Santa Cruz, CA 95061

Notes

Notes

Notes

To Order this Book

Heart, Breath, and Graceful Movement is available for sale at bookstores and can be ordered on the web at:

www.amazon.com

www.wgpublishing.us